THE UNTAMED WORLD

Wolves

RSVP

RAINTREE
STECK-VAUGHN
PUBLISHERS
The Steck-Vaughn Company

Austin, Texas

Published by Raintree Steck-Vaughn Publishers, an imprint of Steck-Vaughn Company.

Library of Congress Cataloging-in-Publication Data
Dudley, Karen.
    Wolves / Karen Dudley.
       p.   cm. -- (The Untamed world)
    Includes bibliographical references (p. 63) and index.
    Summary: Examines the lives of wolves as pack animals, describes their physical characteristics and habitats, and discusses the folklore surrounding them.
    ISBN 0-8172-4561-8
    1. Wolves--Juvenile literature.   [1. Wolves.]   I. Title.
II. Series.
QL737.C22D84   1997
599.74'442--dc20   96-8365
                                      CIP
                                      AC

Printed and bound in Canada
1234567890 01 00 99 98 97

Project Editor
Lauri Seidlitz

Design and Illustration
Warren Clark

Project Coordinator
Amanda Woodrow

Raintree Steck-Vaughn Publishers Editor
Kathy DeVico

Copyeditor
Janice Parker

Layout
Chris Bowerman

Consultants
Carolyn Callaghan, Central Rockies Wolf Project
Dr. Lu Carbyn, Northern Forestry Centre
Dr. John Gunson, Alberta Environmental Protection

Acknowledgments
The publisher wishes to thank Warren Rylands for inspiring this series.

Photograph Credits

Alberta Environmental Protection: page 37; **Tom Brakefield**: page 35; **Corel Corporation**: cover, pages 4, 5, 6, 7, 8, 10, 11, 13, 14, 15, 18, 19, 20, 21, 22, 27, 28, 29, 43, 44, 55, 59, 60, 61; **Glenbow Archives**: pages 41 (NA–544–81), 54 (NA–3394–16); **Ivy Images**: pages 24 (Leonard Rue Ent.), 25, 27 bottom (Don Johnston), 34 (Frank S. Balthius), 42 (J.D. Taylor), 45; **John C. Whyte**: page 16; **Parks Canada**: page 12 (T.W. Hall); **Wilf Schurig**: pages 9, 17, 30, 32; **Tom Stack & Associates**: page 10 right, 23 (Thomas Kitchin), 26 top (Victoria Hurst), bottom (Diana L. Stratton); **Visuals Unlimited**: page 40 (R. Lindholm); **The Wolf Education and Research Center**: pages 56 bottom and 57 bottom (Kathy A. Maechtle), 57 top (U.S. Fish and Wildlife Services).

Contents

Introduction

Savage killer, werewolf, or warrior brother—what does the wolf mean to you?

What is faster than a speeding rhinoceros, can travel through snow for 22 miles without rest, and can smell prey from a mile and a half away? Is it an imaginary superhero? No, it is the wolf. These are just a few of the many fascinating facts about wolves that you will discover in this book.

Find out how wolves can hunt animals that are much larger than they are. Read about how affectionate wolves are toward their pack mates. Follow wolves as they mark out their territory. Learn why wolves howl, and what they mean when they do.

You will also find out why stories like *Little Red Riding Hood* and *The Three Little Pigs* have affected the way we think about wolves. Savage killer, werewolf, or warrior brother—what does the wolf mean to you?

Wolves are fascinating animals, but they mean different things to different people.

Features

One of the wolf's closest living relatives is the domestic dog.

When you catch sight of a wolf, you might think that it looks a lot like a husky or a German shepherd. In fact, one of the wolf's closest living relatives is the domestic dog. Wolves are also related to other wild dogs, such as coyotes, jackals, and dingoes.

Although wolves look a lot like domestic dogs, a closer look reveals many differences between them. A wolf is built for running. It is slimmer than most domestic dogs, and its body and head are longer. Wolves also have longer legs, bigger, blockier feet, and bushier fur. Special features such as these help wolves survive in the wild.

Opposite: Wolves have special features, such as long legs and bushy fur, to help them survive in their environment.

When you compare wolves to some domestic dogs, such as a husky (left), the close relationship between dogs and wolves is clear.

Size

The size of a wolf depends on where it lives. In the northern part of their geographical range, wolves tend to grow larger and have thicker fur and bigger feet. Northern wolves can weigh up to 130 pounds (59 kg), while southern wolves are much smaller, weighing in at about 50 pounds (23 kg). Some wolves in the Middle East may weigh as little as 30 pounds (14 kg).

Including its tail, an average adult wolf can measure anywhere from 4.5 to 6.5 feet (1.4 to 2 m) in length. It can stand 26 to 38 inches (65 to 95 cm) high at the shoulders.

In general, female wolves are about 20 percent smaller than male wolves.

Fur

Most wolves are smoky gray with **tawny**-colored legs and flanks. However, some wolves in Canada and Alaska are jet black. Others in Greenland and the High Arctic tend to be creamy white, sometimes with a bit of pale gray on their backs.

Wolves shed their fur in the spring or early summer to grow a new coat. A wolf's coat has two layers. The first layer is a light-colored **underfur**. These hairs are short, soft, and thick, and they help keep the wolf warm. They contain an oily substance that makes the underfur waterproof.

The second layer is longer fur, known as the **guard hairs**. These hairs are hard and smooth. Whenever a wolf gets wet or dirty, its guard hairs act like duck feathers, shedding the moisture and dirt. In cold weather, these slippery hairs shed moisture so that ice does not collect on the fur. In this way, the underfur is kept dry, and the wolf stays warm. Together, these two layers of fur provide such good **insulation** that a wolf can sleep outside comfortably, even when the temperature dips to -40°F (-40°C).

The name "gray wolf" comes from the color of the wolves' fur. Gray wolves are usually a smoky-gray color, but they may sometimes be black or white. Black, white, and gray wolves can occur in the same litter of wolf pups.

LIFE SPAN

The life span of a wolf in captivity is 11 to 12 years, although some captive wolves have lived for 17 years. Many biologists believe that the life span of wild wolves is much shorter because of the dangers they face.

Special Adaptations

Wolves have several features that are specially adapted to help them survive the challenges of their environment.

A wolf's senses of hearing and smell are very good. These features help make it an excellent hunter.

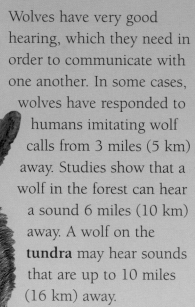

Hearing

Wolves have very good hearing, which they need in order to communicate with one another. In some cases, wolves have responded to humans imitating wolf calls from 3 miles (5 km) away. Studies show that a wolf in the forest can hear a sound 6 miles (10 km) away. A wolf on the **tundra** may hear sounds that are up to 10 miles (16 km) away.

Smell

Wolves have an excellent sense of smell. Using only their sensitive noses, wolves can identify other animals up to 1.5 miles (2.5 km) away. This is often how wolves locate their prey.

Teeth

The wolf's 42 teeth are its most efficient hunting tools. They are sharp, large, and ideal for grabbing and holding on to prey. Their teeth are also very good at tearing meat from bones. With its sharp teeth and strong jaws, an adult wolf can crack open bones to get to the marrow that is inside them.

A wolf's teeth are larger than the teeth of any kind of domestic dog.

A wolf's long legs and large feet allow it to pursue prey over different kinds of landscapes.

Legs

Wolves are often on the move for 8 to 10 hours a day. Long, muscular legs allow wolves to move easily through unbroken snow or rushing water. They can travel for miles without stopping. One biologist in British Columbia, Canada saw two wolves run through deep snow for 22 miles (10 km), without once laying down to rest.

Paws

A Russian proverb says that "a wolf is kept fed by its feet." When you look at a wolf's paws, you can see why this is true. While it is hunting, a wolf must be able to run over long distances. Its legs are long, and its feet are big and blocky—perfect for running. These large feet are like snowshoes, evenly distributing the wolf's weight across ice and snow. When a wolf is traveling over uneven surfaces, it can spread its toes far apart to grasp rocks or logs. With its large paws, a wolf can chase caribou across the flat tundra, or it can follow wild sheep up a rocky slope.

Classification

Species

There are two main species of wolves in North America, the gray wolf (*Canis lupus*), and the red wolf (*Canis rufus*). Most North American wolves are gray wolves. Red wolves were once almost extinct, but conservation efforts have now begun to restore their numbers in the wild.

SUBSPECIES

At first, biologists thought there were 24 subspecies of gray wolves in North America. Based on where the animals lived, scientists drew lines marking the range of each subspecies. When biologists began studying wolves in more detail, they discovered that wolves often crossed over these boundaries. Some even traveled right through the ranges of other subspecies. Now, most biologists believe that there are only four subspecies of the gray wolf living in North America. A fifth subspecies is believed to be extinct.

Latin Name	Where They Live
Canis lupus lycaon	Southeastern Canada
Canis lupus arctos	High Arctic
Canis lupus occidentalis	Northwestern Alaska and Canada
Canis lupus baileyi	Mexico, Texas, and Arizona It is almost extinct in the wild.
Canis lupus nubilus	Believed to be extinct

Ancestor, or Hybrid?

Red wolves are smaller and have different features than gray wolves. Although scientists believe the red wolf is a separate species, they have two theories about its origin.

The first theory involves **genetic testing**, tests that examine genes to find out an animal's origins and its relationship to other animals. These tests have shown that the red wolf may be a **hybrid**, or a cross between a gray wolf and a coyote.

The second theory comes from looking at fossils. Scientists who have examined wolf fossils believe that red wolves are actually the ancestors of gray wolves. According to this theory, red wolves first evolved in North America. Some of these wolves then left and traveled over the Bering Strait into Europe and Asia. Over a very long period of time, they adapted to their new environment and evolved into a new species, the gray wolf. These gray wolves then traveled back into North America, where they took over the territories of the remaining red wolves.

The first theory would explain why red wolves look like both gray wolves and coyotes. The second theory would explain why there are more gray wolves than red wolves in North America. Scientists are still debating the two theories.

Coyote

The Pack

Wolves live in groups called packs that are very similar to human family groups.

Opposite: When food is scarce, a wolf pack is always on the lookout for intruders in their territory.

Despite stories that describe wolves as lone, savage creatures, wolves are actually very friendly, social animals. They live in groups called packs that are very similar to human family groups. The size of a pack can range from two to about twenty wolves, but most packs have five to twelve members. Living in a pack allows wolves to hunt large prey and raise their young within the protection of a group. The packs are **territorial**, which means they will defend their area from other lone wolves or from packs of wolves. Within their territory, each pack lives, hunts, and raises their pups.

Wolves often play with their pack mates. They jump around and chase one another, often getting as much exercise as when they are hunting.

Composition

The wolf pack is a family of wolves that usually includes a mated pair and their offspring. At times, a close relative may also join the pack. The pack increases in late spring each year with a new litter of pups. After the first year, a newly formed pack can have six to nine members. The pups stay with the pack until they mature. A well-established pack may include adult members and half-grown wolves as well as newborn pups. After the young wolves are full-grown, some individuals **disperse**, or leave the pack, to find mates and start their own pack. This way, the pack does not get too large. Sometimes older offspring will stay with their original pack as long as there is a lot of food. As soon as prey becomes scarce, however, the older offspring disperse.

Wolf packs usually have five to twelve members, though a pack may have up to twenty members if food is abundant.

Formation

A pack forms when a lone male in search of a mate meets a lone female looking for the same. If the wolves like each other, they court by wagging their tails, touching noses, and snuggling together. This type of behavior is called pair-bonding. Pair-bonding can take place at any time of the year.

The mating season occurs during late winter or early spring. Until the female is ready to mate, the pair spends their time together hunting and playing. At the same time, they also search for vacant territory. Ideally, this territory will include a lot of prey, a good location for a den, and a reliable source of water. Sometimes lone wolves will look for a suitable unoccupied area before seeking a mate.

A courting pair of wolves are very affectionate toward each other.

Function

A wolf pack's main function is to make sure that its members survive the dangers and difficulties of their environment. Wolves depend on larger prey to survive. A pack can catch large prey more easily than a single wolf. The pack also serves as a safe place for pups. As young wolves mature, they watch and imitate the adults, learning by example how to survive in their environment.

By living within the protection of a pack, wolves are better able to survive in their environment.

Organization

A wolf pack is organized by rank. The **alpha**, or top-ranking, male and female are mates who dominate all other members of the pack. Middle-ranking, or **beta**, wolves dominate lower-ranked animals, who in turn dominate the **omega**, or lowest-ranked wolf.

A wolf's rank is often related to its age. The oldest wolves are called the alphas. Next come the oldest offspring, the **yearlings**, and then finally the newborn pups.

The alpha wolves dominate all the other pack members. The alpha wolves also guide the whole pack. They decide where to go, when to hunt, and which prey to attack. They are the first to feed when the pack makes a kill, and they are usually the only wolves in the pack to mate. When a pack travels in the winter, the alpha wolves are first in line, blazing the trail for the smaller, weaker wolves.

Seasonal Activities

Throughout the fall, winter, and early spring, the pack travels together, hunting and marking their territory. This all changes in the late spring with the birth of the pups. When pups are born, the pack's life revolves around the den. Even though the adults still go off to hunt, they return to the den every few days to socialize. During these spring and summer months, wolves often hunt alone. In the warmer weather, small prey is abundant. This makes it easier for the wolves to hunt separately. If and when the wolves get lonely, they can always find their pack mates by returning to the den.

During spring and summer, wolves sometimes hunt alone. In the fall, winter, and early spring, wolves usually travel with their packs.

Communication

Wolves have many ways of communicating. Just like humans, they make faces to show their moods. If a wolf is happy, its ears are forward, and its mouth is open with its tongue hanging out. A threatening face has a wrinkled nose with an open mouth and bared teeth.

Wolves also communicate by howling. Wolves howl to regroup pack members, to warn off other wolves, and to signal the beginning of a hunt.

Scent marking is another way that wolves communicate. To establish a pack's territory, or to communicate with other pack members, the alpha male, or sometimes the female, will lift its leg and urinate on a distinct spot. This spot is known as a **scent post**.

Body Language

When an alpha wolf needs to show its rank to another wolf, it makes a threatening face. It raises its hairs and tail, puffing itself up so it looks bigger. The lower-ranked wolf closes its mouth, flattens its ears back, and tries to make itself look smaller. It lowers its body and puts its tail between its legs. The lower-ranked wolf may even lie down and roll over in submission. Sometimes an alpha wolf just glares at a low-ranked wolf. Under this stare, the other wolf cringes and slinks away.

Pack members often greet one another affectionately. Playing is an important part of the wolf's social life because it helps pack members bond.

Scent Marking

A scent post is usually located on a bush, log, rock, or large snow clump. Scent posts often mark the pack's territory and let intruders know that the area is occupied. There may be twice as many marks around the edges of a pack's territory as there are in the center of it. Scent posts may also mark kill sites. The markers can last for weeks.

Howling

Although howling is an important way for wolves to defend their territory and communicate with other pack members, it is also a way for wolves to socialize. In the morning, the entire pack greets one another affectionately and begins to howl. If a member has wandered away, it comes running back at the first call, eager to join in the group song.

Wolves may howl while they are standing up, sitting, or lying down.

Public Wolf Howls

In the 1950s, scientists began studying wolves in Algonquin Provincial Park, in Ontario, Canada. In order to locate the packs, biologists imitated wolf howls. The wolves howled back. Soon this method of finding wolf packs became standard practice.

Since 1963, Algonquin park naturalists have offered public wolf howls. The wolf howls are held in August, after the pups have grown enough to leave the den. If the weather is good, naturalists take people out on Thursday nights and imitate wolf howls by the side of the highway. If wolves are in the area, they may howl back. The program has attracted people from all over the world. So far, almost 100,000 people have visited the park just to hear the wolves howl.

Wolf Pups

The entire wolf pack helps raise the pups.

Wolf pups are born in late spring, when prey is most abundant. The birth is an exciting occasion for the whole pack. The father and the other pack members crowd around the den, wagging their tails. The new pups are greeted with excitement and happy whines. In the weeks to come, the entire wolf pack helps raise the pups. Adult pack members will bring food back for the new mother and her pups, or they will watch the pups while the mother goes hunting.

Wolf pups are very curious about their world. They learn how to survive by watching everything around them.

The Den

The mother wolf begins searching for a den months before the birth. Wolves will often dig at many places before deciding where the den should be. The den must be close to drinking water, and it must offer protection for other pack members. Most dens are in forested areas, because most wolves live in the forest. If danger threatens, the other pack members can hide among the trees. Sometimes the same dens are used every year.

A mother wolf will hollow out her den if the soil is soft and easy to dig.

If the soil is soft and easy to dig, the mother wolf hollows out her den. Wolves prefer underground dens, although they may also use a crevice in a rock pile or a hollow log. They may even use an abandoned beaver den. The den's nesting area is located at the end of a long tunnel. The nesting space is usually uphill from two or more separate entrances. This helps protect the nesting area from flooding if there are heavy rains.

Birth

The **gestation period** for wolves is 63 days. Pups are usually born in late April or early May in northern regions, and mid-March to mid-April in the southern regions. The average litter size is five to six pups and can be as many as eleven. Weighing only 12 to 16 ounces (.3 to .4 kg), the pups measure 10 to 13 inches (25 to 33 cm) in length. Their coats are short, fuzzy, and dark brown or blue-gray in color. The pups are born blind. They also cannot hear very well because their ears are folded over their foreheads. At this time, the pups are entirely dependent on their mother for warmth and food.

Care

Other pack members help the mother with her pups. When the mother goes hunting, another wolf will care for the pups until she returns. This wolf is usually fed by the other pack members who will also take turns feeding and playing with the cubs.

Pups nurse four to five times a day for periods of 3 to 5 minutes at a time. After the pups are **weaned**, the adults feed them by carrying food back to the den in their stomachs, and then **regurgitating** it for them.

When the young pups see the adults returning from a hunt, they run up to them eagerly. By nipping at an adult's cheeks and mouth, the pups try to get it to regurgitate. The pups' actions trigger the regurgitation reflex in the adults.

Adult wolves carry back food for the pups in their stomachs.
The adults then regurgitate the food for the pups.

Development

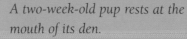

A two-week-old pup rests at the mouth of its den.

Weeks 1 – 5

After the first week or two, the pups open their eyes, and their ears begin to straighten. They start to explore their den. If they wander too far, their mother will bring them back quickly. After 3 weeks, the pups begin to get their baby teeth. By the fifth week, their mother starts to wean them. At this point, they are able to eat tiny pieces of food that the adults have regurgitated.

Weeks 6 – 10

After 8 weeks, the pups have their adult teeth and weigh about 15 pounds (6.7 kg). They start to grow their adult hair around their noses and eyes. At this time, the pups are moved to an aboveground den where they can romp and play. These sites are usually near rock crevices or in sheltered forest areas. The pups stay close to the site when the adults are hunting. If danger threatens, the pups squeeze into the crevices or hide among the trees for safety.

A five-week-old pup practices howling.

Weeks 11 – 15

As the young pups continue to grow, they start to imitate the adults' hunting techniques in their play. When the wolf pups are older, these hunting techniques will be essential to their survival.

By week 11, pups begin to acquire the body shape of adult wolves.

Weeks 16 – 20

After about 16 weeks, the young wolves begin traveling and hunting with the adults. Even though they are almost full-sized, the young may stay with the pack for 2 to 4 years. During this time, they learn how to survive in their environment. Young wolves are not ready to mate until they are two to three years old. By this time, they have usually dispersed to establish their own territories and packs.

By the time a pup is 16 weeks old, most of its fuzzy baby fur has been replaced with adult hair.

Habitat

Wolves can live wherever there are enough large prey animals for them to eat.

Opposite: Although most wolves live in the forest, they can be found in many other kinds of habitats.

A habitat is an area that provides food and shelter for an animal. Wolves can live in a wide variety of habitats. They may be found in rocky mountains, valleys, thick forests, or on the arctic tundra. Wolves can live wherever there are enough large prey animals for them to eat.

A wolf's habitat may affect its behavior. For example, northern wolves are well adapted to colder weather and may sometimes change their habits to avoid hot temperatures. As the weather warms up in the summer, these wolves hunt only at dusk or at dawn. They spend the rest of their day cooling off in a shady forest, even if they have not managed to hunt successfully. Wolves living on the tundra, which is a treeless plain, like to get away from the hot sun by lying in the shade of shrubs or low hills. When wolves lie down to sleep, they leave a dent, or depression, in the grass or shrubs. Sometimes, clumps of fur are also left behind. These spots are known as bedding sites.

Many of the wolf's prey live in or around ponds and marshes. In order to hunt these animals, wolves have learned to be comfortable in water.

Wolf Territories

Within a habitat, a wolf pack establishes its **home range**, or territory. This is the area where wolves live and hunt. The size of these territories can vary a lot, depending on the amount of prey that is available. Where prey populations are dense, wolves do not have to go as far to get a meal. In harsher habitats that support fewer prey animals, wolves may have to travel for long distances before making a kill.

In addition, the prey animals' range can affect the territory claimed by a wolf. Herds of caribou often roam over great distances, but deer usually stick to a smaller area. Wolves that prey on caribou can have ranges of over 1,000 square miles (2,600 sq km), while packs that prey on deer may cover territories of only 30 square miles (78 sq km). David Mech, a biologist with the United States Fish and Wildlife Service, studied a pack of wolves in Alaska that covered 5,000 square miles (13,000 sq km) in 6 weeks.

Wolves do not constantly patrol their home range. They may pass through a corner of their territory only a few times a year.

Musk oxen live in the harsh environment of the far north. Wolves that prey on musk oxen claim large territories, because their prey must travel long distances to get food.

Viewpoints

Should we control wolf populations to increase the size of big game herds?

An important part of a wolf's diet are large animals, such as caribou and elk. These animals are known as big game animals by people who like to hunt. Some people argue that wolves kill too many big game animals. In order to control wolf populations, they suggest that wolves should be trapped or killed. Other people believe that wolves should be left to live and hunt in their habitat without human interference, and that wolves kill just enough prey to keep their habitat's ecosystem balanced.

PRO

1 Fewer wolves mean more big game animals for humans to hunt or study.

2 If big game populations are low because of bad weather or loss of habitat, wolves will keep their numbers even lower by preying on them. If wolves are trapped or shot, the prey populations will have a chance to recover.

3 When food is scarce, wolf pups die slowly of starvation and disease, and adults may end up killing one another in competition for food. Wolf controls mean a healthier wolf population.

CON

1 When wolves hunt, they prey on the weak or vulnerable. In this way, wolves strengthen big game herds by leaving the strong animals to breed.

2 Wolves control their own numbers by allowing only the alpha wolves to breed. In addition, younger adults disperse from packs that are too large.

3 Studies of caribou herds show that some herds increased with wolf controls, and others increased without the controls. The effectiveness of wolf controls varies depending on many factors.

On the Track of a Wolf

You will probably never see a wolf in the wild. They are shy of humans, and can hear or smell your presence long before you might see them. Even if you are not lucky enough to see a wolf, there are a few ways that you can tell if one is in the area:

1. Tracks that look like a dog's but are generally larger, up to 6 inches (15 cm) across. The middle two toe prints are usually **parallel** to each other.

2. **Scat**, or feces, that is tube-shaped like a dog's, but contains hair from the wolf's prey.

3. Scent posts, usually tree trunks, stumps, or rocks that a wolf has marked with urine to outline its territory. These are easiest to see on the snow during the winter.

4. Dead animals, such as deer, elk, or moose that have been partially eaten.

5. The howling of a wolf or wolf pack. Wolves usually howl in the evening to signal the beginning of the hunt. You also might hear them calling to one another early in the morning.

Wolf tracks look similar to dog tracks, but are much larger.

If You See A Wolf...

If you are lucky enough to see a wolf, watch it closely. Wolves show their emotional state through body language. If you know enough about wolf communication, you can tell how each wolf may be feeling. Here are a few tips:

I am an alpha wolf.

Let's play!

I am a low-ranked wolf.

Stay away!

33

Food

Although wolves have been known to eat grasses, fruits, and even mushrooms, they must hunt other animals to survive.

Opposite: If a wolf has gone without food for a few days, it may eat up to 13 pounds (6 kg) of meat in one day when it finally makes a kill.

Large prey can be difficult to hunt. For this reason, wolves also hunt smaller animals, such as rabbits.

Wolves are **carnivores**, or meat-eaters, which means that their ideal food is meat. Although wolves have been known to eat grasses, fruits, and even mushrooms, they must hunt other animals to survive. Wolves will catch and eat smaller prey, such as mice and rabbits, but they prefer to hunt larger animals, like deer, caribou, or moose so they will have food for a longer time. Some studies show that up to 98 percent of a wolf's summer diet is from prey larger than the size of a beaver. In the winter, this number is even higher. Unfortunately for the wolves, hunting for large prey is often unsuccessful. Large prey can be aggressive or hard to find. Sometimes a wolf will go for a whole week without catching anything to eat.

What They Eat

What a wolf eats depends on where the wolf lives. Northern wolves hunt moose, caribou, musk oxen, and bison. Wolves in the forest eat deer and elk. In the mountains, wolves hunt wild sheep. Sometimes wolves will kill a large animal in excellent health. More often it is the weak, young, or old animals that are killed. A sick or old animal is easier to catch, so wolves travel long distances to find such animals. Although wolves rely on hoofed mammals for their main source of food, they will also eat beavers, porcupines, hares, rabbits, snakes, and birds, such as ducks, grouse, and geese. In fact, wolves will hunt just about any kind of animal. For a light snack, a wolf may even snap up a small mouse or vole. When their natural prey is scarce, a wolf may also hunt cattle and other domestic animals.

Wolves hunt many different kinds of prey, including (from left) moose, elk, musk oxen, caribou, mice, and rabbits.

How They Hunt

Wolves can hunt alone or in a pack. It is possible for a lone wolf to kill a large animal, although larger prey are usually hunted by the whole pack. Wolves locate their prey by scent and then try to sneak up on the animal. As the wolves get closer, they try to get their prey to run. They know that a running animal is more vulnerable and less likely to kick and injure them. When pursuing prey, a wolf can reach speeds of 45 miles per hour (72 kph). It may take hours or even days to make a kill.

Wolves attack the rump area first. As soon as the prey is stopped, some of the hunters grab the animal by the nose. At the same time, others bite the animal's flanks, neck, and throat. The prey is down in minutes.

Once the prey has been brought down, the whole pack moves in to get their share of the kill.

Prey is usually still alive when the wolves begin to eat. The leaders tear open the animal's stomach to get at the soft organs inside. These organs are very rich in fat and nutrients. Other pack members try to bite meat from the wounded areas. Snarling and growling, each wolf tries to guard its share of the kill. If the prey is very large, the wolves eat as much as they can, and then bury chunks of meat in **caches** for later.

Prey that refuse to run usually survive a wolf attack, because the wolves are wary of sudden charges and sharp hooves. When prey stands its ground, the wolves surround the animal and lie down. Every so often, one or two of the pack leaders will get up and walk closer to see if they can panic the animal into running. If the animal does not run, the wolves will soon leave to search for an easier meal.

The Food Web

Each living thing pictured below belongs to a food chain. A food chain shows how energy, or food, is passed from one living thing to another. The arrows point to the direction in which the energy moves. For example, plants are food for a rabbit, which is food for a wolf. Every animal survives by eating plants or animals in its food chain.

A food web is made up of many food chains. In a food web, a living thing can belong to a number of different food chains. As you can see from the food web drawn below, wolves belong to numerous food chains. How many food chains in this web would be affected if wolves disappeared?

Wildlife Biologists Talk About Wolves

Dr. David Mech

"I hope I can help other people see the wolf for what it is: one more magnificent species, superbly adapted to contend with its harsh environment, and highly deserving of our understanding and acceptance."

Dr. David Mech is known as the "Wolf Guru" or "Wolf Man." Since 1958, he has been studying wolves in Canada, the United States, and Italy. Dr. Mech has written hundreds of articles and is the author of *The Wolf*, and *The Arctic Wolf: Living with the Pack*.

Diane Boyd

"Sometimes the wolves [seemed to] play jokes on us. One morning, we skied up the river...the wolves were about 4 miles north and we were going up to track them. When we came back, a pack of twelve wolves had come down the river on top of our ski tracks, in broad daylight."

Diane Boyd is a wolf biologist working for the University of Montana's Wolf Ecology Project. She lives near Glacier National Park, where she is able to study the return of wolves to the Northern Rocky Mountains.

Peter Clarkson

"[Wolves] are so individualistic. It is almost like the study of people. You get some wolves that are helping out all the time. Other wolves just laze around. Some wolves go off traveling. Other ones keep to themselves. Even within a pack you get real different personalities."

Peter Clarkson is a Canadian wolf biologist who has studied wolf-caribou relationships in the Northwest Territories in Canada.

Competition

Evidence shows that wolves succeed in catching and killing their prey only 7 to 10 percent of the time.

Opposite: It can take many hours or even days for a pack to make a kill. Wolves will snarl and growl at one another to guard their share of the food.

A wolf's life is a difficult one. Living in a wild environment, the wolf must compete with other wolves for both food and territory. Hunting prey can be dangerous and is often unsuccessful. Evidence shows that wolves succeed in catching and killing their prey only 7 to 10 percent of the time. Once a wolf manages to bring down its prey, it must then guard its kill from other predators or scavengers looking for an easy meal. These same predators will also attack and kill wolf pups, so wolves must guard their young at all times. Finally, wolves must also compete with humans, who are by far the wolf's worst danger.

In their search for food and territory, wolves compete with other wolves, wild animals, and humans. Competition with humans has usually meant death for the wolf throughout history.

Competing with Other Wolves

While wolves compete with their pack mates for food or rank, these encounters rarely lead to serious injury. Occasionally, however, they can lead to death. When a pack's alpha wolf has been injured or has grown too old to lead the pack, the next dominant wolf will become the leader. Sometimes the old alpha wolf does not want to give up its position. When this happens, the two wolves fight for the leadership of the pack. In some cases, the old alpha wolf may even be killed.

When wolves compete with other wolves for territory, however, the fights are often deadly. If a pack finds another pack or a lone wolf on their home ground, they chase the intruders and attack them. If they can, the wolves kill the strangers. In areas where there is plenty of prey, however, wolves are far more tolerant of one another. They may even have friendly relationships with wolves from other territories.

Competition for food among wolves can be vicious, but it rarely leads to wolf deaths.

Competing with Other Animals

During their travels, wolves often encounter other predators. Usually the wolves win these competitions. In the western part of North America, for example, both wolves and cougars hunt the same prey. In most direct encounters, the cougar backs off, retreating to a high tree branch. This may be because the cougar, which is a solitary hunter, is outnumbered by the wolf pack. Sometimes, however, the encounter leads to a fight. Although wolves and cougars usually avoid one another, wolves have been known to follow cougar tracks in order to steal the cat's kill. Coyotes try to do the same thing to wolves, but the wolves are larger and can usually chase off the coyotes or kill them.

In competitions between wolves and bears, the two animals are evenly matched. Bears may take over a wolf kill or kill a wolf, but wolves may kill bear cubs. Studies in Alaska and Canada have found that grizzly and black bears are the wolf's main competitors other than humans.

Most North American cougar populations are too low to be serious competitors of wolves. Magpies and ravens, however, can eat up to 25 percent of a wolf's kill.

Competing with Humans

As human populations spread into wild areas, wolves are forced into competition with humans for territory and food. When their natural habitat is destroyed, wolves are forced into other areas. Sometimes these other areas support fewer prey. In addition, human hunters compete with wolves for prey animals. If prey is scarce, the wolves may hunt livestock in order to survive.

Sometimes ranchers leave their dead livestock on the edges of their farms. The wolves eat these dead animals and develop a taste for domestic animals. When wolves start hunting livestock, ranchers start calling for wolf controls, which are programs that allow people to kill wolves in a variety of ways.

Increasing human populations are forcing many wolves into areas where their natural prey are not abundant.

Challenges to Wolf Survival

When European settlers came to North America, they killed many of the wolf's natural prey. As their natural prey disappeared, wolves began hunting domestic animals. To protect their livestock, the settlers did everything they could to kill wolves. They used guns, traps, and poisons, and they dug up dens. Cowboys put poison on dead animals they found, and government "wolfers" specialized in killing wolves. During this wolf control campaign, wolves disappeared from most of the United States, Mexico, and parts of southern Canada.

Humans are just one of the possible dangers that a wolf will face in its lifetime. In addition, wolves can be kicked or trampled by the prey they are chasing, especially if the animal is much larger than they are. This is the cause of most wolf injuries. Wolves can also be injured by rockfalls or by broken, jagged trees. They often pursue their prey across rivers, so they also run the risk of drowning in swift-flowing water. Finally, if prey numbers are low, some wolves may starve to death.

Many ranchers believe that wolves are a danger to their livestock. Often humans kill the wolves after first catching them in leghold traps.

Folklore

Folktales and stories often reflect the feelings people have about wolves. In stories from hunting societies, the wolf was a divine creature, admired for its hunting skills. In stories from agricultural societies, where wolves posed a threat to livestock and farms, they were a menace. Stories and legends are still told of greedy, evil wolves preying on helpless humans. Werewolf movies, for example, are modern versions of very old stories.

Science has done a lot to disprove the myth of the evil wolf. The more we learn about wolves, the less dangerous they seem. Still, the influence of stories like *Little Red Riding Hood* and *The Three Little Pigs* can be very powerful.

Folklore History

The ancient Greeks believed that the wolf was a ghost animal that could make people speechless with its stare. In ancient China, the wolf was a symbol for cruelty. Early Christians believed wolves were savage, wicked creatures that were friendly with the Devil.

However, not everybody saw wolves in such a negative way. There are tales told in many cultures of wolves raising abandoned human children. Soldiers in Ancient Rome who were going into battle saw the wolf as a good omen because it was a follower of Mars, the god of war. The North American Pawnee viewed the wolf as a kind of warrior brother. In their stories, the wolf taught them how to hunt buffalo, and to share the kill with their community.

Myths vs. Facts

Wolves howl at the full moon.

Wolves do not howl at the moon, full or not. They howl to warn other packs of their presence or to communicate within their pack.

Wolves are greedy hunters that kill more than they can eat.

Wolves are not greedy, although they will sometimes gorge on a kill. This usually occurs when food has been scarce. If there is leftover meat from a kill, the wolves may bury the meat in a cache and eat it later.

Wolves kill humans.

Sometimes people are killed by sick or captive wolves, but nobody in North America has ever documented a fatal attack on a human by a healthy, wild wolf. In fact, wolves that live in the wild are afraid of people and often run away from them. Even when biologists have taken pups from a den, the adult wolves do not attack.

Wolves will adopt abandoned children and raise them with their own pups.

Stories about a wolf raising a human child have been told in many cultures since ancient times. In the twentieth century, these tales have even appeared in newspapers, magazines, and textbooks. Despite this, there is not one proven case of this myth.

Folktales

The folktale wolf can be evil and dangerous, or helpful and kind. Some wolves may be quite clever, while others are very foolish and are often tricked by people or other animals. There are so many folktales about wolves that it is almost impossible to list them all. Here are just a few you might enjoy:

Helpful Wolves

"The Twins of the God Mars" tells the story of two brothers, Romulus and Remus, who are abandoned by their evil uncle. A female wolf finds them and raises them with her own pups.

Toor, Frances. *The Golden Carnation and Other Stories Told in Italy*. New York: Lothrop, Lee & Shepard Company, Inc., 1960.

Wolves take in an abandoned girl and care for her. When she is grown, the girl returns to her people and teaches them the wolves' custom of caring for those who cannot hunt.

Matson, Emerson. *Legends of the Great Chiefs*. Nashville: Nelson, 1972.

Funny Wolves

Learn the story of The Three Little Pigs from the wolf's point of view.

Scieszka, Jon. *The True Story of the Three Little Pigs*. New York: Viking, 1989.

Magical Wolves

"The Firebird" tells the story of Prince Ivan, who must find the firebird and rescue a beautiful princess. He is helped in his quest by a magical wolf.

Wyndham, Lee. *Russian Tales of Fabulous Beasts and Marvels*. New York: Parents' Magazine Press, 1969.

In "The Wolf's Eyelashes," the eyelashes of a wolf will give magical sight.

Novak, Miroslav. *Fairy Tales from Japan*. New York: Hamlyn, 1970.

Evil Wolves

In this story from China, a wolf tries to eat three children by pretending to be their grandmother.

Young, Ed. *Lon Po Po*. New York: Philomel Books, 1989.

"Iron Wolf" is the story of a wolf that agrees to help a man, but asks a terrible price in return.

Wiggin, Kate Douglas. *The Fairy Ring*. New York: Doubleday, 1967.

In "The Wolf's Food," the evil spirit, Kurat, creates the wolf with dire consequences.

Maas, Selva. *The Moon Painters and Other Estonian Folk Tales*. New York: Viking, 1971.

Foolish Wolves

In "The Wolf's Breakfast," a wolf is tricked by a goose.

Zajdler, Zoe. *Polish Fairy Tales*. Chicago: Follett, 1959.

"The Groundhog Dance" tells the story of a groundhog that teaches the wolf how to sing and dance.

Bell, Corydon. *John Rattling Gourd of Big Cove*. New York: Macmillan, 1955.

How and Why Stories

Find out why the wolf has a short tail in "How the Wolf Lost His Tail."

Montgomerie, Norah. *Twenty-five Fables*. New York: Abelard-Schuman, 1964.

In this story, a wolf dives into a lake trying to get a blue coat, with unexpected results.

Parker, Arthur Caswell. *Skunny Wundy: Seneca Indian Tales*. Chicago: Albert Whitman, 1970.

Threatened and Endangered Wolf Populations

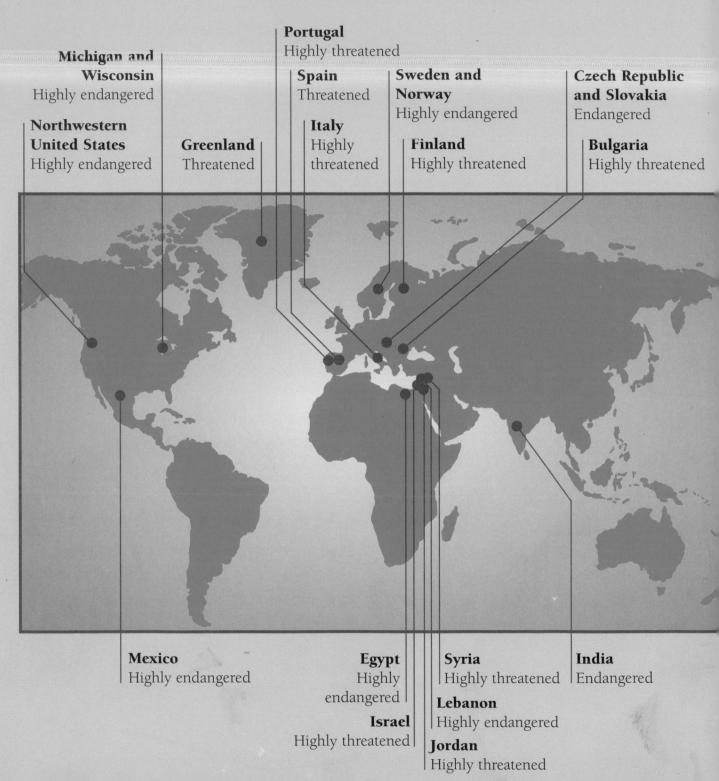

Portugal
Highly threatened

Michigan and Wisconsin
Highly endangered

Spain
Threatened

Sweden and Norway
Highly endangered

Czech Republic and Slovakia
Endangered

Northwestern United States
Highly endangered

Greenland
Threatened

Italy
Highly threatened

Finland
Highly threatened

Bulgaria
Highly threatened

Mexico
Highly endangered

Egypt
Highly endangered

Syria
Highly threatened

India
Endangered

Lebanon
Highly endangered

Israel
Highly threatened

Jordan
Highly threatened

Status

At one time, wolves had the largest range of all land mammals except humans.

In 1992 wolf biologists from all over the world gathered together in Edmonton, Alberta, Canada at the International Wolf Symposium. Many scientists had suspected that wolf populations were in trouble. The Symposium was held to determine the status of wolves worldwide. The news from countries varied.

At one time, wolves had the largest range of all land mammals except humans. As human populations grew, some of the wolf's habitat was destroyed to make room for farms and cities. Sometimes wolves left these areas and moved into more remote regions. When the wolves stayed around, they were often hunted and killed.

WORLD STATUS OF WOLVES

...ABLE	VULNERABLE	THREATENED	ENDANGERED	EXTIRPATED	EXTINCT
...pecies that is ...le to survive ...d reproduce.	A species that is at risk because of low or declining numbers.	A species that is likely to become endangered due to habitat loss, persecution, or declining numbers.	A population that is in danger of becoming extinct or extirpated.	A species that no longer exists in a certain area, but may be found somewhere else.	A species that no longer exists anywhere.
...ska, Alberta, ...orador, ...nitoba, ...skatchewan, ...nnesota, ...rthwest ...ritories, Ontario, ...ébec, Yukon, ...tish Columbia, ...n, Poland, ...ssia	Afghanistan, Arabian Peninsula, Greece, Mongolia, Romania, Turkey	Bulgaria, Finland, Greenland, Israel, Italy, Jordan, Portugal, Spain, Syria	Mexico, Michigan, Wisconsin, Northwestern United States, Czech Republic, Egypt, India, Lebanon, Slovakia, Sweden, Norway	Newfoundland, Southwestern United States, Central Europe, Hungary	

Conservation Status

Most of the wolf populations in Europe and Asia are in decline because of human activity. In many countries, habitat loss has forced wolves to live in areas where humans also live. In some of these regions, the wolf's natural prey is extinct or scarce. Wolves in these regions sometimes live on scraps from garbage dumps. At other times, they prey on pets or livestock. When this happens, the wolves are hunted down and killed. Many countries now have laws to protect wolves, but these laws can be difficult to enforce. Even where the protection laws are successful, wolf populations may be too small to breed successfully.

In many European countries, wolves are already extirpated. The largest wolf populations in Europe and Asia are in Mongolia, which has about 10,000 wolves, and in Russia, which has about 70,000 wolves. Unfortunately, many people in these countries still see wolves as savage killers, so they still hunt wolves.

Wolf controls are no longer widely practiced in North America, although both the Alaska and Yukon governments have recently run programs to increase hunting opportunities for humans. There are about 6,000 wolves in Alaska and 40,000 wolves in Canada.

In the early part of the century, official wolf control programs wiped out wolf populations in many parts of the world.

Reintroduction Programs

Over the years, wolves have disappeared from much of their historical range. Without wolves as predators, the hoofed animal populations in many of these areas have grown too large. Hoofed animals, such as deer, elk, and buffalo, survive by eating vegetation. If their populations grow too large, the vegetation in their habitat is overgrazed. Overgrazing results in a shortage of food, especially during the winter. When winters are harsh, many hoofed animals die of starvation.

A balanced ecosystem has many different kinds of plants and animals, including predators such as wolves.

Wolves are part of a healthy ecosystem. They help improve the health of hoofed animal herds by weeding out the weak and sick. They also help by reducing the size of herds that are too large. Smaller herds mean that overgrazed vegetation has a chance to grow back. Animals killed by wolves also provide food for scavenger species, such as ravens. For these reasons, biologists have developed programs to reintroduce wolves into their historical territory.

Reintroduction programs involve both captive and wild wolves. In some programs, captive-bred wolves are released into the wild. In other programs, wild wolves are trapped and transferred to reintroduction areas.

These programs are not popular with everyone. Some people are afraid their livestock or pets may be killed by wolves. Others worry that wolves will prey on threatened species, such as wild sheep. Despite this opposition, reintroduction programs are now under way in Mexico and the United States.

Sponsorship

Many wildlife experts believe that the future of wolves depends on what people think about them. To help people better understand wolves, scientists study wolf packs to learn more about the wolves and their behavior. You can help by sponsoring a wolf from one of these packs.

The Wolf Education and Research Center

One of the places you can sponsor a wolf is at the Wolf Education and Research Center, in Idaho. In partnership with the Nez Perce tribe, biologists at the Center have created a home for the Sawtooth Wolf Pack. The pack lives at the Center in a 15-acre (6-ha) forested enclosure.

Although these wolves are in captivity, they are not pets. Jim Dutcher started the Sawtooth wolf project in 1990. Jim did not want tame wolves at the Center. He wanted to study the behavior of wild wolves. He worked hard to build a careful relationship with the Sawtooth pack. He wanted the wolves to be comfortable around humans, but he also wanted them to behave as wild wolves do. Jim's hard work has paid off. The Sawtooth wolves are comfortable around the sight and scent of humans, but they still behave as a wild pack with their own rules. Biologists can now study the pack easily, and visitors to the Center can experience wolves in their natural habitat.

This biologist is attaching a radio collar to a wolf. The collar sends out radio signals that the biologists use to keep track of the wolf's movement across its territory.

Reintroduction Sponsorship

You can also help by sponsoring wolf reintroduction programs. In a joint project between the American and Canadian governments, wild wolves are being brought back into their traditional territories in the United States. Each year for five years, about thirty Canadian wolves will be transferred to the United States. The project's goal is to have ten wolf packs in Idaho, ten in Montana, and ten in Yellowstone National Park, in Wyoming.

Wolves are transported in pens before being released into their new area.

In the first step toward reintroduction, Canadian biologists go out in helicopters to trap wolves and attach radio collars to them. This allows biologists to track the wolves' movement. They can then locate the wolves quickly when it is time to transfer them to the United States. The wolves are always moved in the winter. This gives them time to explore their new territory before the pups are born in the spring.

After they are caught, the wolves are flown to the area where they will be released. There they are placed in pens for a few days. This allows them to recover from the trip and get used to the new area. When the wolves are ready, they are released into their new home.

For more information about these programs, you can write to the Wolf Center at:
Wolf Education and Research Center
P.O. Box 917
Boise, Idaho
83701

What You Can Do

By learning more about wolves, you can make better decisions about how to help them. Subscribe to a wolf publication, or join a conservation group and find out how you can help.

Publications

"International Wolf"
International Wolf Center
1396 Highway 169
Ely, MN
55731-8129
Phone: 1-800-ELY-WOLF

"Wolf"
P.O. Box 29
Lafayette, IN
47902-0029

Alberta Environmental Protection
9915 – 108 Street
Edmonton, Alberta
T5K 2G8
Canada

Conservation Groups

INTERNATIONAL

Wolf Haven International
7447 Boston Harbor Rd. NE
Olympia, WA
98506

World Conservation Union
World Conservation Centre
Avenue du Mont-blanc
CH-1196 Gland
Switzerland

Society for the Protection of Wolves
53902 Bad Münstereifel
Von Goltstein Street #1
Germany

CANADA

World Wildlife Fund Canada
90 Eglington Ave. E.
Suite 504
Toronto, Ontario
M4P 2Z7

UNITED STATES

International Wolf Center
5930 Brooklyn Blvd.
Suite 200
Brooklyn Center, MN
55429

North American Wolf Society
P.O. Box 82950
Fairbanks, AK
99708

The Wolf Fund
P.O. Box 471
Moose, WY
83012

Wolf Haven International
3111 Offut Lake Rd.
Tenino, WA
98589

Twenty Fascinating Facts

1 A wolf has five toes on each front foot and four toes on each hind foot. The claw on the fifth toe, located above the foot pads, is known as the **dewclaw**. Dewclaws can become quite sharp and curved. A hunting wolf uses these curved claws to help hold struggling prey.

2 Some gray wolves change color and get lighter as they grow older. Each time they molt, the wolves' fur changes slightly in shade and tone. One captive black wolf changed to light gray by the time he was eight years old.

3 Wolves have extremely powerful jaws and teeth that can crack bones and tear meat. The wolves like to crack bones open so they can get to the nutrient-rich marrow that is inside.

4 Wolves have a good sense of smell and can recognize another pack's territory by their scent posts. If wolves smell the scent post of a strange wolf, they urinate to cover the smell with their own scent.

5 During regular travel, wolves move at 5 to 9 mph (8 to 14 kph), but they can speed up to 35 to 43 mph (56 to 72 kph) for short distances. If necessary, a wolf can travel over 20 miles (32 km) without a rest.

6 Wolves have to work hard for their meals. Most of their main prey animals have evolved defenses against them. A deer can outrun a wolf or injure it with a kick of its sharp hooves. Caribou usually stay in groups for protection and defend themselves with pointed antlers. Moose can outrun a wolf, although they usually stand their ground and try to kick any wolves that come near.

7 Wolves are very good swimmers. During the hunt, they may occasionally swim across rivers or lakes. A wolf can catch and kill an animal while swimming.

8 Wolves control their numbers through domination. The alpha wolves will not permit lower-ranking wolves to mate and produce offspring.

9 Wolves love to play. When a wolf is feeling playful, it raises its tail slightly, pricks its ears forward, and bows to its pack mate while raising a front paw. Then it crouches down. If its companion wants to play, it will jump forward, and the two wolves run, jump, and roll over each other. Often other pack members will join in the fun.

10 While they are eating, wolves make many trips to nearby water to drink and to wash the blood from their coats.

11 While hunting, wolves sometimes roll in dead animals that they find. This behavior is not well understood. The stench of the dead animal may hide the wolves' natural smell that might alert prey to their presence.

12 Wolves have definite personalities. Top-ranking wolves are confident and outgoing, while low-ranked wolves tend to be shy. Even within these social roles, each wolf shows distinctive traits, such as playfulness or laziness.

13 Wolves are very affectionate and often seek physical contact with their pack mates. They nuzzle, nip, and cuddle with one another, especially if they are mated.

14 Wolves howl to warn off intruders or to communicate with members of their own pack. They can howl while they are standing, sitting, or lying down.

15 In addition to scent marking their territory, wolves also mark empty food caches. When a wolf digs up a cache, it urinates in the empty hole to let its other pack members know that the meat has been taken.

16 If a mother wolf is killed, a female pack member will raise her pups. This substitute mother can even produce milk to feed them.

17 Wolves sometimes return to use the same den each year. In the High Arctic, there is one cave that wolves have been using as a den for 700 or 800 years.

18 Adult wolves regurgitate food for their pups. The wolves carry food back to the den, where the pups wait eagerly. The adult can regurgitate at least three times in one trip.

19 Wolf pups play at dominating one another. One will act like a dominant wolf and stand over another. As they continue to play, however, the other pup will try to dominate the first.

20 Wolf population numbers remain low because they continue to be hunted and killed by humans, and because of habitat loss.

Glossary

alpha: Something that is first. In wolf packs, an alpha wolf is the top-ranked wolf.

beta: In wolf packs, beta wolves are middle-ranked wolves.

cache: A hiding place that is used for storing food

carnivore: An animal that eats mainly the flesh and body parts of other animals

dewclaw: The claw located on the fifth toe of a wolf's front paws

disperse: When a young wolf leaves its maternal home range

genetic tests: Tests that examine genes to discover the origin or development of a species

gestation period: The length of time a female is pregnant

guard hairs: The long, smooth hairs of a wolf's coat

home range: The entire area in which a wolf pack lives

hybrid: The offspring of two animals of different species, races, or breeds

insulation: A barrier that keeps heat from entering or leaving

omega: Something that is last. In wolf packs, the omega wolf has the lowest rank.

parallel: Having sides equally distant from each other

regurgitate: To bring up food that has not been fully digested

scat: An animal fecal dropping

scent posts: Distinct areas like small bushes, rocks, logs, or clumps of snow that wolves urinate on to outline their territory

tawny: A golden-brown color, sometimes with a hint of red

territorial: Being protective of one's home range

tundra: A treeless plain in the northern Arctic

underfur: The soft, thick hairs of a wolf's coat. They are shorter than the guard hairs, with an oily substance that makes the hairs water-resistant.

wean: To stop feeding a pup milk and start feeding it solid food

yearling: An animal between one and two years old

Suggested Reading

Brandenburg, J. *White Wolf: Living with an Arctic Legend*. Minocqua: North Word Press, 1988.

Busch, Robert. *The Wolf Almanac*. New York: Lyons & Burford Publishers, 1995.

Busch, Robert, ed. *Wolf Songs*. Vancouver: Douglas and McIntyre, 1994.

Carbyn, L.W., S. Fritts and D. Siep. *Ecology and Conservation of Wolves in a Changing World*. Canadian Circumpolar Institute. Edmonton: University of Alberta, 1995.

Lawrence, R.D. *Trail of the Wolf*. Toronto: Key Porter Books, 1993.

Lopez, Barry H. *Of Wolves and Men*. New York: Charles Scribner's Sons, 1978.

Mech, L.D. *The Arctic Wolf: Living with the Pack*. Stillwater: Voyageur Press, 1988.

Mech, L.D. *The Way of the Wolf*. Stillwater: Voyageur Press, 1991.

Mech, L.D. *The Wolf: Ecology and Behavior of an Endangered Species*. Minneapolis: University of Minnesota Press, 1970.

National Geographic Video. *White Wolf*. Washington, D.C.: National Geographic Society, 1988.

Savage, Candace. *Wolves*. San Francisco: Sierra Club Books, 1988.

Index